3413

Oboe Classics

FOR THE

Advanced Player

FOR

OBOE

AND

PIANO

Music Minus One

MMO

3413

Contents

ᔑᔐ

Suggestions for using this MMO edition

WE HAVE TRIED to create a product that will provide you an easy way to learn and perform concerted music with accompaniment in the comfort of your own home.

Where the soloist begins a movement *solo* or without an introduction, we have provided an introductory measure with subtle taps inserted at the actual tempo before the soloist's entrance.

Chapter stops on your CD have been notated in the score as well as in the index. This should help you quickly find a desired place in the music as you learn the piece.

Regarding tempi: we have observed generally accepted tempi, but some may wish to perform at a different tempo, or to slow down or speed up the accompaniment for practice purposes. You can purchase from MMO specialized CD player/recorders which allow variable speed while maintaining proper pitch. This is an indispensable tool for the serious musician and you may wish to look into purchasing this useful piece of equipment for full enjoyment of all your MMO editions.

We want to provide you with the most useful practice and performance accompaniments possible. If you have any suggestions for improving the MMO system, please feel free to contact us. You can reach us by e-mail at info@musicminusone.com.

©2007 MMO Music Group, Inc. All rights reserved.
ISBN 1-59615-360-1

Dear Fellow Oboists and Teachers,

I chose these works because they are particular favorites of mine. They are playable by advanced high school or college-level oboists, but they could form the centerpieces of a professional recital. The Verroust pieces are little known, but there is nothing more fun to play! As a special bonus for your performing convenience this album includes a separate booklet containing the printed piano accompaniment scores for these pieces, as they are nearly impossible to find.

My involvement with Music Minus One has shown me that it is a first-class educational tool. I've heard my twelve-year-old horn-playing daughter play her favorite pieces over and over with the piano track, building her strength without even realizing it. Often when you practice and become tired, you just stop, but with a pianist to urge you on, you can stretch yourself and build endurance.

Imitation is a perfectly valid way to learn style and good taste. What you put in your ear comes back out, and students should take care that what is fed in will lead to their goals! In general, students need to listen to more music. The more music you know by a given composer, the more understanding you will bring to the rest of his works. The most important music for the oboe is the orchestral repertoire. Find a library that circulates CDs, and start with the symphonies of Beethoven and Brahms, then go down the Table of Contents in your excerpt book. A serious high school oboist should be familiar with the tempi, context and style of the major symphonic works. If you order a full part, you could even play along.

Another great value of Music Minus One is to help your intonation. The only way for an orchestra to play in tune is for individuals to train so that they can start AND END at the same pitch, just as they would play a recital with piano. To say an orchestra *will* rise in pitch as it goes along is NOT ACCEPTABLE, and people who say this are just caving in to bad habits! Having a pianist and an in-tune A=440 piano is great practice for you to maintain a stable pitch center for any ensemble you're in! You could just play with a tuning box sounding the key of the piece, but that's not much fun!

Last, but not least, it's really fun to have instant accompaniment. When I play elementary or Junior High School concerts, I no longer need a teacher to learn my accompaniments, tune the piano, or even *have* a piano; I just ask for a CD player! It works great! I picture myself some day in my old age, playing Verroust for fun with Mr. Nielsen!

I'd like to dedicate my work on this project to my teacher John Mack, who continues to challenge and inspire me and who instilled love and devotion for teaching.

I would also like to thank Erik Nielsen, not only for accompanying me like a mind-reader, but for his generous and expert help editing the text for all three volumes.

—*Elaine Douvas*

Notes on the Music

Georg Friedrich Handel

Everybody knows Händel: the guy who wrote *Messiah*, with its splendidly inspired "Hallelujah Chorus," but did you know that Händel wrote over 40 Italian operas that lay in neglect for 200 years? The stories are about kings and queens of ancient history: their human sufferings, love intrigues and moral dilemmas. He also wrote 25 oratorios in English, which are operas in all but name. They were often performed with scenery and costumes, but their religious subjects were forbidden to be acted on stage. Händel was born in Germany (1685-1759), studied in Italy, and lived most of his life in England. The list of his complete works covers 22 pages of fine print! The oboe sonata is impossible to date accurately, but was probably written in his early twenties in Italy. What Händel learned from the Italian opera composers was absolute mastery of the technique of writing long-breathed, rhythmically flexible melodies for the voice. The Italian influence softened his German angularity, but both elements are present in this beautiful sonata. When playing Händel, remember that he was mainly a composer for the theater. His music should not sound dry and objective; it should be approached with a keen sense of human emotion and drama.

Oboe Sonata in g minor (op. 1, no. 6)

1ST MOVEMENT

Vocal quality should be the first goal in presenting the *Larghetto*. Many things go into playing as singers sing, but smooth legato of wind and fingers and really shapely, curving slurs are at the top of the list. The slurs need *portamento*, Italian for "carried over," a slight scoop-shape for upward slurs and an arch-shape on downward slurs. The very first interval is of immense beauty; be sure that it has enough reach and travel and please, no C-key on the high B♭; extra keys not in the fingering destroy the breadth and resonance of a note, making it sound squashed and metallic. (Regarding finger action, see my nots for Verrout No. 3.)

It is important to stress the proper notes in the theme: the first note to aim for is the high A in measure 2, followed by a soft D. D will tend to stick out because it's a long note and overly powerful note. This same strong A/weak D pair occurs in measure 6 and measure 11. The E-flat on measure 3 should be stressed and melt into a softer D. All of the trills should begin on the upper note, which is an *appoggiatura*, a melody note that is dissonant with the chord of the moment. Play these dissonances with expression and emphasis, then the resolution is felt as relief, repose.

The piece begins in g minor, but there is a constant dialogue of minor and major, giving it a mood of wistful optimism and nobility. It is not a sad piece. Be sure to react to all modulations in music; a change of key is like traveling to another land. Here, specifically, you must play the major cadences with warmth and confirmation. Forget about the editor's printed *diminuendo* at measure 7; you've traveled to A major! You could highlight the rich and unexpected B-natural in the minor-ninth chord in measure 14 with a change to delicate tone color.

This beautiful work presents a formidable challenge to the oboist's endurance. If the reed does not hold itself up in the high notes, you will tire your face jamming the pitch up, and get too much pressure in the sound. The tone throughout should be unforced, floating and buoyant, light and mobile to convey the spiritual elevation of the line. The reed should have a built-in "pitch floor," that is, a point below which the pitch cannot drop. This is a function of very tight sides that press against each other all the way to the top and enough "stoppage" behind a tip that is not too long. Then you can actually voice *down* on the high notes for fullness, keeping the jaws apart.

The dotted rhythms need to be played with special character: the dotted sixteenth and thirty-second figure should be "double-dotted," that is, change the thirty-seconds to sixty-fourths, making the figure sound snappy, lilting and angular. In the dotted eighth and sixteenth figures, the sixteenths should remain as full, sturdy sixteenths.

In Baroque music, when you have a trill on a tied or dotted note, try to stop the trill squarely on the tie, replacing the motion of the trill with *vibrato* on the tie. Don't let the trills go too fast for the mood of the piece.

The first movement ends on a dominant chord (D major) and needs to resolve to the home key of g minor when the second movement begins, therefore, do not take too much time or clean your instrument between movements. The ear is waiting for the g-minor resolution.

2ND MOVEMENT

The *Allegro* is a temperamental contrast to the fragile first movement. Its mood is imperious with strong rhythm and accents on all four beats; the strongest of the accents is the one felt on the tie. Händel was Beethoven's favorite composer; what Beethoven would have liked here is the rhythmic vitality, the muscularity, the harmonic clarity and simplicity. Play the bouncy eighth and quarter notes with sturdy tone and attack, still keeping a vocal quality in the articulation; not too much tongue noise and with a little curve on the ends of the notes like saying "m." Think 98 percent tone and 2 percent tongue-noise. Try to match the eighth note lengths to each other, as it is unstylish to elongate the last in a series of *staccato* notes (e.g. measure one and the end of measure three). In the mixed articulation, take care that two basic rules apply: all the notes should be equally heard, and the even rhythm should be unaffected by the

slurred groups. It is common for slurs to rush and notes not tongued to sound weak. The cross fingerings of the F-major *arpeggio* are really difficult. Curved fingers, light finger action and a lot of practice are probably the key! I like a lilting effect in the syncopated pairs of eighth notes at the top of the second page: strong-weak-strong-weak with no real space between them. Play the trills starting right on the beat with the upper note.

3RD MOVEMENT

The short melody of the *Adagio* is so beautiful in its unadorned simplicity. It is sincere and expressive, honest and frank. There is a noble striving, ending with poignant resignation. I would not call it stark or incomplete, and I feel no great need to decorate it. It sounds like a vocal recitative, a passage between arias where text is conveyed against simple chords in the accompaniment. If you do opt for filling in the intervals with ornamentation or added melody notes, be careful not to trivialize or cheapen the melody. The patterns should not be predictable or singsong, trite or repetitious. These are surely the emotions of kings and queens; the regal expression must be retained. I'm compelled to quote my teacher John Mack, "Use only the finest perfume, and not too much of it."

4TH MOVEMENT

In the time of Händel, composers did not specify exactly what articulations to use. You are at liberty to choose the tonguing and slurring patterns, but whatever you choose, the tonguing should take nothing away from the tone. In the figure: tongue 1, slur 2, the tongued note should sound like a bow-stroke, not dry and clipped, but a little broad, with the same amount of bow that the two slurred notes would take together. In the six-note slurs, try for continuity: define the attack without clipping the end of the previous group. Tongue late and fast; the tongue simply urges the tone forward. A slur is not a phrase mark; it's just a smooth bow change. No "hiccups" in between!

The rhythm should have a dance-like swing, but the mood is turbulent and stormy, a sort of *furioso*. Let the sequence of ascending scales accumulate. The large leaps (sixths and sevenths) are emotionally charged, just as they are in the first movement.

Breathing and fatigue can be a big problem here, especially after playing the other three movements. Even though I can do circular breathing, I chose to demonstrate how one might deal with the non-stop motor-rhythm of notes by leaving out one or two to accommodate a fast breath. I indicated which notes I left out by parentheses in the oboe part. I think this is an acceptable solution, but you still must learn to take very quick, unobtrusive breaths without any gasping noises!

Stanislas Verroust

Louis-Stanislas-Xavier Verroust (1814-1863) is not a famous composer; he's not even listed in the comprehensive Grove's Dictionary of Music and Musicians, but what delightful music he wrote! Verroust was the professor of oboe at the Paris Conservatory from 1853-1863. In those days it was the custom for a teacher to compose a new piece each year for the students' July *Concours*, or competition. If you were one of the 2 or 3 oboists per year recommended for the *Concours*, you could win a First Prize, Second Prize or First or Second Honorable Mention. Once you attained a "First Prize" you were out, graduated from the Paris Conservatory, even if you were only 15 years old like Georges Gillet, author of the "Gillet Etudes."

Verroust got his First Prize in 1834, when he was 20. He held many important posts including one as a second violinist in the *Theatre du Palais Royal*! He was principal oboe of the Paris Opera from 1839-1855, and this certainly had a deep influence on his style of composition. He wrote over sixty Fantasies and Variations on operatic themes, described in the French *Biographie Universelle des Musiciens* (1837-1844) by F.J. Fétis (vol. 8) as tasteful, graceful and elegant. Verroust's oboe playing is described by Fétis as fine, delicate, and expressive. The composer Berlioz, in his amusing book *Evenings with the Orchestra*, speaks of the Beethoven Festival organized by Liszt and Spohr in Bonn, where he was appalled at the poor quality of the oboe playing. He says sarcastically, "What a great tragedy if, in place of the bad oboist, for example, who had played the solos with such mediocrity, one had brought Vemy or Verroust from Paris, Barret from London, or Evrat from Lyon, or any other player of sure talent and excellent style!" Unfortunately Verroust descended into severe alcoholism, lost all of his positions and died a premature death at the age of forty-nine. (Barret of London is the man who wrote the Barret *Oboe Method*.)

Verroust composed twelve *Solos de Concert*, also called *Concertos*, for oboe and piano. Originally there was string orchestra accompaniment for the *Concours*, but the orchestrations are lost, except for nos. 1, 8 and 9 in the Paris Library.

Each "Solo" is composed of 2 or 3 linked movements, like a scene from an opera: one or two slow arias and a flashy ending. Verroust shows off the oboe's beauty of sound in the various registers and elegant *bel canto* ("beautiful singing") ornamentation.

Solo de Concert No. 2 (1855)

No. 2 in g minor begins with a dramatic "orchestral" introduction to set the stage. You can play the printed notes of the introduction if you want; it might help you get warmed up for the first attack of the *Andante*, which must emerge poetically. The atmosphere has veiled mystery, urgency and intensity. Let the *vibrato* evolve, bringing breadth and warmth to the tone as you color each successive D with more layers and dimension, echoing away the last one. The *vibrato* must confirm, not confuse the pitch and stay within the tone outline. It must not be jagged or formulaic. Like a fine singer, the tone should have sufficient scope and weight to carry the musical idea. It must have resonance, ring, outline, focus, clarity and depth. The soft tone should sound open and ringing; it must not be squeezed, muffled, bitten or missing its high overtones. The louds are obtained by permission and not by force.

We are trying to achieve a floating effect, buoyant and unpressured. I don't think you can get this by playing on an empty little reed and relaxing. Playing the oboe is about as "relaxed" as a ballet dancer. It must *look* and *sound* relaxed, but it involves some strong opposition of muscles to give the tone body, resonance and outline. The trick is to make the pressure against yourself, against a focus spot or concentrator in the throat, at a safe distance away from the reed, so that nobody can *hear* pressure. You can find this spot in the throat by saying "young" or by gargling! Support is not how much you blow, but how you hold the air. It's sort of like using your thumb over the end of a garden hose. I love this analogy: if you wanted to water the flowers six feet away, you wouldn't turn the water up full blast and knock all the petals off the flowers. You would keep the water amount moderate and use your thumb to get a traveling, aerated stream, concentrated and of some width. This is how you get a big tone that sounds effortless, clear, floating, and well projected.

The style of this piece is "operatic." This means there should be great flexibility in rhythm of the melody called *rubato*, Italian for "robbed." You stretch some notes and make up the time by hurrying others. The rubato should take place basically within the steady tempo of the accompaniment. In opera, rhythms are often interpreted for dramatic effect rather than exactly subdivided ("rhetorical" versus "literal" rhythm). For example, in line 4, all of the single sixteenth notes are played late with an imperious snap directed at the long notes. A singer will sometimes choose to highlight a high note with extra length or to show off the dynamic range with a *messa di voce* (literally "placing the voice."). This means ornamenting a note by making a *fermata* and traveling the entire dynamic range *pp <f> pp*, such as the D at the end of line 3 or the *fermata* D in line 6. (Hold the *fermatas* one extra beat to stay with the piano). Another of my teachers, the flutist Marcel Mouse, would say about the high-point of the phrase, "If zee note eez good, KEEP, KEEP!" It's part of the operatic style.

All of the grace notes in this slow part should be played very melodically: on the beat, slowly, and tongued so as to highlight their poignant dissonance. They are *appoggiaturas*.

The *Mosso moderato* is a *Polacca*, Italian for a piece, or originally a dance, in Polish style with ¾ time and stylized rhythm. Verroust was in Paris during the same time as Chopin (who died in 1849), and Polish things had become very fashionable. The Polacca evolved into a brilliant, ornate instrumental showpiece. The dotted rhythms should be as snappy as possible: play the thirty-second notes as late as you can and lightly, almost parenthetically. Let them coast along as you connect the long notes to each other. On page two, the step-wise pairs marked *dolce* should lilt, that is, each pair should diminish, and the printed rests just indicate a tiny lift. The air, and therefore the abdominal muscles, must be in motion: loud-soft, more air-less air, alternating tight and loose to get the dynamics. You can't do this with a stiff or constant support. Lilting is a function of the air; it can't be done by mouth.

I have interpolated a high-note ending, which is a custom to add brilliance. This is show-off music, so it's appropriate to the style.

PAUL HINDEMITH

Paul Hindemith (1895-1963) was born in Germany, but he moved to America, taught at Yale (1940-53), and became an American citizen in 1946. He wrote a sonata for almost every instrument, including trombone, double bass, and harp! He wrote seven operas.

I have found in my years of teaching that many students have misconceptions about Hindemith and tend to play his music too heavily, neglecting the composer's lyrical, melodic qualities. Hindemith's style is "neo-classical" and "contrapuntal." That means he wrote complementary, architecturally constructed, independent lines similar to Bach. Clarity and line are essential to bring out the counterpoint. Avoid stereotyping German music as heavy: the Oboe Sonata has nothing to do with the German army of World War II! The first movement appears in the Intermediate volume of this series.

II. SEHR LANGSAM (VERY SLOW)

The second movement opens in a contemplative mood, with a beautiful, sustained, searching melody. There is a misprint of the metronome mark, because the oboe part says 54, and the piano part says 63; I prefer the 54. Make a nice arch in the first fragment, which is very consonant, serene and comforting. Round off the second F gently, as a phrase ending. Feel the striving, searching and mystery in m. 3, sustaining the tension as the F-B♭ interval pulls to B♭, a tritone. Start the answering half of the phrase just as loud as the first half arrived; this is a general rule for achieving really satisfying symmetry. The search is wearying, and the melody falls down with breathless interjections from the piano. The lines over the eighth notes don't mean just "long;" they indicate to give individual expression to each, a sort of weight accent and curve away ("m"). The surprise major harmony ("Pic-

cardy Third") on the last note (D#) is like a refreshing oasis. As interpreters it is our job to create the pain and take it away, so that the listener fully experiences the music's tension and relief, discord and reconciliation.

The upbeat to figure 1 should be a little louder than the sudden pianissimo. Then a longer and more purposeful search is undertaken. Bring out the upper notes and minimize the repeated As as the phrase struggles to reach the summit. The breaths belong before the G# and not again until after the climactic high D♭, as there must be one coherent effort to attain that height. Again it falls down, sighing away on the syncopated E and settling into a reassuring major chord. There is a great deal of mystery and urgency in the thirty-second notes after Figure 2. The climactic major chord one measure after Figure 3 is absolutely victorious.

LEBHAFT (LIVELY)

The joyous fast theme is, of course, the same melody, played faster ("diminution.") The 3-note pick-up motif needs energy and wind-up. Curve away from each quarter note like a bell-tone ("m" or *forte-piano*). Clip the notes short before the accents to maximize the syncopation; it needs a lot of throw and catch. Feel the rhythm strongly on all of the ties, and bring out the single sixteenth notes, placing them precisely.

The rhythm at figure 5 is really difficult. The thing that throws you off is that the piano is playing a waltz-like "oom-pah-pah," but the accent is always on beat 3, not beat 1. I admit that I get through this section solidly by submitting to the piano's accents and feeling the oboe part as syncopated. I

do a little re-barring in my mind, and I put hooks (V) and triangles (△) in my music to show the piano's groupings of twos and threes. After the nightmare of trying to play this when I was 15, this method is, for me, secure and well understood!

The chorale melody at Figure 7, which will ultimately end the work, is soaring and majestic. Reach for the G#, and resolve a little to F# before crescendoing on to the A. In general, the line and the large architecture are more important than such smaller nuances, but within the large direction there should be curves, consonant sounds and resolutions of expressive dissonances. It is not necessary to maintain a constant "aah" syllable to get a line! Use a singing, vocal attack and note length for the eighths. The important ending motif (B♭-E♭-D-B) is mysterious at first and triumphant at the fortissimo. The long diminuendo on B is very exciting; overload the note with more air than it can take and gradually blow less and less, adjusting the throat focus to keep the tone potent, unsqueezed, and in tune. If you bite for diminuendos, you will go sharp.

At *Sehr langsam, wie zuerst* (Very slow, as at first) the piano has both the melody and the mysterious accompaniment while the oboe comments wistfully. Try to capture the inflections of speech in the repeated pitches. You will need lots of curve in the notes ("m"on the ends) and very flexible support.

The *fugato* at "Again lively" is intricate and exciting the way the theme piles on itself. The measured push to the end is inexorable. Over-hold the accents in the fourth and fifth measure of Figure 18 with total joy. The bell-tone dotted quarters are as if every church bell in town is ringing. It ends in a blaze of glory. The mystery and contemplation, the soaring and striving melodies and the joyous heroism of this piece are uplifting and ennobling. I think it is one of the greatest works written for our instrument.

HOWARD HANSON

Hanson (1896-1981) was born in Wahoo, Nebraska, of Swedish ancestry. He was a neo-Romantic composer, who cited Sibelius and Grieg as major influences on his work. He was the director of the Eastman School of Music from 1924-64. Through his position there he was able to shape the musical style of several generations of American composers and musicians. His output includes seven symphonies, five symphonic poems and two operas.

PASTORALE, OP. 38

The *Pastorale* was composed in 1949 for the UNESCO Chopin Centennial Concert in Paris. (Chopin died in 1849.) Hanson dedicated it to his wife, whom he married in 1946. The original version is for oboe and piano, but Hanson arranged the accompaniment for string orchestra and harp in 1950, and it was premiered by the Philadelphia Orchestra with Marcel Tabuteau as the soloist.

There is an atmosphere of mysticism in the opening section, expressive of infinity or outer space. For five lines, every phrase ends questioningly. The tritones and sevenths are unsettling, as are the wandering half steps that never resolve. After the fiery scale to high C#, a catharsis is finally reached at the 5/8, breathless and spent. Feel the swing of the three plus two like waves lapping a shore. The eerie feeling also comes from Hanson's use of the "octatonic" scale, a scale that alternates whole step/half step/whole step/half step, etc. The first few notes of this pattern appear often, foreshadowing what is to come. At the end, the part that sounds like a crisis (*Più animato*) ends with a complete octatonic scale.

The large leaps and downward slurs are really challenging. All the slurs need an "active" shape; don't let them just fall out, especially the downward octaves. Try aiming upward instead of straight down at the note, sort of like a swan dive. The shape should be arched as if going over a waterfall: out first, then down. Bring the air to a crest at the end of the upper note. Then, at the last minute before changing notes, practically stop blowing as you go to the

(continued on page 24)

Sonata II
for Oboe and Piano

Georg Friedrich Händel

4 taps (1 measure) precede music.

SOLO OBOE

8

4 taps ♩.
(1 measure)   ↓ ④ 22
precede music. **Allegro**

2ᵉᵐᵉ Solo de Concert
for Oboe & Piano

Edited by
Elaine Douvas

Stanislas Verroust, op. 74

Mosso moderato

Sonate
for Oboe and Piano

II.

Paul Hindemith

Sehr langsam, wie zuerst

MMO 3413

14

↓ 10 28

Wieder lebhaft

dim.

To Peggie

Pastorale
for Oboe and Piano

Howard Hanson op. 38
Composed for Chopin Centennial
UNESCO Paris 1949

Escales No. II
"Tunis-Nefta"
for Oboe & Piano

Jacques Ibert

a son Elève Fernand Magnien

3me Solo de Concert
for Oboe & Piano

Edited by
Elaine Douvas

Stanislas Verroust, op. 74

20

Moderato

MMO 3413

(continued from page 5)

lower note. This gives a lot of vocal content to the interval.

I want to say a word about the registers on the oboe. It is very important that the lower the note, the deeper, longer and more forest-colored the tone should become, and vice-versa; the high notes should become stronger and more brilliant. I am concerned about shallowness in the low G and thinness of high B and middle C in the first phrase. Try two exercises: first, play A-G-A-G etc., making sure it goes "ee-oh-ee-oh," not "oh-aing-oh-aing." Bs and Cs are notoriously thin and bare on the oboe. Make an exercise of this too: B-C-B-C etc. in the middle register, trying to thicken and match the tone and get a small half step of pitch. Keep experimenting until the C is the same color as the B. Do it by ear, but you might try going to the tip of the reed, opening the jaws, and "overloading" or funneling extra air against the focus in the throat. The opposition of lipping down and wind-ing up gives breadth and content to the tone. Go openly and fearlessly to the high B. Don't back away; it needs body!

"Pastorale," meaning an idyllic country scene, seems an odd name for such an intense and mysterious piece. The trilling section is ominous and becomes more and more dire. Only the *Poco meno mosso* is warm and reassuring. This section has that distinctive "American" sound that we associate with the music of Copland (listen to *Appalachian Spring* or *The Winter's Passed* by Barlow (Intermediate Music Minus One). It comes from the open 4th and 5th intervals that conjure up the spacious prairies of the West, pioneer spirit, honesty and bravery. It has the sweetness and simplicity of a church hymn. Don't let the low Ds stick out, and use nice arched downward slurs. When you get to the dramatic climax (*più animato*), don't play the sixteenths too short; a broader *staccato* gives more tone. The end is a sort of transfiguration: restful, tranquil, at peace.

JACQUES IBERT

After serving in the French army during World War I, Jacques Ibert (1890-1962) won the *Prix de Rome* in 1919. This prize, awarded every year from 1803 to 1968, gave a composer a four-year, totally paid stay at the Villa Medici in Rome just to study and compose! While in Rome, he wrote *Escales* ("Ports of Call,") a three-movement orchestral tone-poem depicting his steamship sojourn to three Mediterranean ports: Palermo, Tunis-Nefta and Valencia. It is his most popular piece. Toward the end of his career, Ibert composed an oboe concerto called *Symphonie Concertante* (1948).

ESCALES NO. 2 "TUNIS-NEFTA"

Oboes always get these great exotic, Oriental solos! This is a very useful piece to know. School audiences love it; the kids always ask me for "the snake-charmer piece." Kids are also intrigued when I use circular breathing in the trills, however, I don't think this is the most musical way of playing the piece. This solo is often asked at professional orchestra auditions because it offers much scope for the imagination and is a formidable test of low-note control, intonation, dynamic range and finger technique.

Tunis is the capital of Tunisia on the northern coast of Africa. Nefta is an inland city to which Ibert must have journeyed. The metronome mark is by the composer, and his French words mean, "moderate, very rhythmic," "soft-textured and melancholy." Always look up any words you don't know!

Play the solo to evoke steamy Africa, perhaps a dancer with a jewel in her navel—very insinuating. You could give a separate wind to each eighth note to make it sound elusive. Taking a little rubato on the exotic augmented 2nd (Bb-C#) adds to the Arabian character. The re-take of the low D is

very difficult to finesse: end the first one by pronouncing an "m;" this will make a lift without actually stopping the note. Sing it to yourself, and you'll see. The loud repeated Fs need big curves in them, almost like forte-piano, to exaggerate the syncopation. "Syncopation" comes from the Latin word *syncopare*, which means "to faint or swoon." The French words mean "with a little intensity in the expression." The high E can be tongued, as it is really a written-out French grace note, accented on the beat. Use the full fingering for high E; there really are no reliable fake fingerings for this. The *tremolo* from Bb to C# is fingered by trilling both fingers of the left hand so that the C# is played with just the index finger of the right hand. Note that there are t7o Bbs in a row where the *tremolo* begins.

When you play the cadenza with the piano track, you will need to figure out when the piano is going to re-enter. You will hear two taps, signaling the end of the A-Bb trill and establishing the tempo of the eighth notes in the last cadenza bar. The breath mark is like two added eighth rests. When the *cadenza* begins, the pulse is in quarter notes. Give four pulses to the *tremolo*. As part of the *ritardando*, the pulse changes from quarters to eighths. That is why there appear to be four beats in the ¾ bar of A-Bb trill.

The reprise says "far away" and "hardly any sound."

VERROUST - SOLO DE CONCERT NO. 3 (1856)

Number 3 in F major begins with a "barcarolle," an elegant Venetian boat song in 6/8 that imitates the gentle rocking of a gondola. Over this floats the sweet and flexible oboe melody, spinning and refined. Be sure the long notes connect well to the start of the moving notes, and reach for the upper neighbors expressively. Try to make the low notes as gentle and fluent as possible, especially the low F, which tends to "roar."

The fingers must be curved in the trills so they will sound liquid and not percussive. In general, the fingers must move quietly, sneakily and curved, with a gentle squeezing action. Straight fingers can be heard as jagged, angular note changes. Try picking the fingers up a little before sneaking them down; if you keep them too close to the keys, the only way to get them down is to snap them. The oboe must cover well, so that the keys don't have to be hit for response. The *fermata* on D (bottom of p.1) is the perfect place for a *messa di voce*. (See Verroust No. 2)

The *Moderato* is full of intrigue, like an opera scene. Tongue all of the grace notes, even when they are under a slur. This is almost always a good idea: for clarity, because they are harmonically interesting, and to differentiate a grace note from a dotted rhythm.

The C-Db trill is fingered by trilling the left hand index finger. It can be tuned perfectly by adjusting the height of the half-hole key. Please do not use the second trill key, intended for Bꞔ-C# trills; it is completely out of tune on C-C#. If you find it difficult to trill the tip of your index finger while holding the side octave key, trill with your middle finger on the half-hole instead. I move to this position between the two Bbs; it works great.

The *Allegro vivo* is such a catchy tune! It sounds almost "flamenco" with the rhythm of clicking heels. The arrogant *rinforzando* notes followed by the aloof suavity of the *subito piano* reminds me of the way flamenco dancers stamp their feet and then stare penetratingly at each other. Grab the B ꞔ a little early to give it more verve. Following tradition, you can interpolate your own high-note ending.

If you like these works, the Solo No. 4 is in *The Oboist's Concert Album* along with other "Concours" solos. It is the blue collection edited by Albert Andraud, published by Southern Music. I think the delightful music of Verroust calls for further investigation!

—Elaine Douvas

MUSIC MINUS ONE
50 Executive Boulevard
Elmsford, New York 10523-1325
800.669.7464 U.S. ← 914.592.1188 International

www.musicminusone.com
info@musicminusone.com

MMO 3413   Pub. No. 00847   Printed in Canada